The Book of Sammy

The Book of Sammy

Written by Sam Doty

Copyright © 2025 by Kr38 Creative, LLC

All rights reserved.

No part of this publication may be reproduced, stored in a retrieval system, or transmitted in any form or by any means—electronic, mechanical, photocopying, recording, or otherwise—without the prior written permission of the publisher, except in the case of brief quotations used in critical reviews or articles.

ISBN: 979-8-9929960-3-6 Paperback
  979-8-9929960-4-3 Hardcover

First Edition

www.kr38iv.com/publishing

For mom, who taught me to put others first —
just by doing it every day.

Foreword:

I didn't write this book to convert anyone. I didn't write it to destroy anyone's faith either. I wrote it because after 44 years of life — most of them spent orbiting Christianity in one form or another — I realized that the version of Jesus most people are selling… doesn't look like the one I remember learning about. This isn't a theology. It's not a system. It's not a sermon. It's a conversation. One human trying to make sense of religion, power, love, doubt, and what remains when you burn off the bullshit. You don't have to agree. You don't have to believe. But if you've ever looked at modern Christianity and thought, "This can't be it…" then you're exactly who this book is for.

I'm not a preacher. I'm not a theologian. I'm not even particularly religious anymore.

But I grew up in church. I played drums in the worship band. I sang the songs, listened to the sermons, even went to a Christian college where they made you take theology classes whether you liked it or not.

And somewhere along the way, I started to see the cracks.

I started to notice the parts of the Bible that didn't get talked about.

The verses that got twisted. The fear that got preached. The money that got passed around. The way Jesus slowly disappeared behind doctrine, rules, judgment, and branding.

The way the name "Christian" got weaponized to mean straight, white, conservative, patriotic, obedient, tithing, judgmental — but not necessarily kind.

This book is my response to all of that.

It's not about telling you what to believe. It's about laying out what I've seen — and giving you permission to say, "Yeah… that doesn't feel right."

This isn't me claiming to have all the answers.

This is me owning the fact that I've lived through a lot of the questions.

And now I'm ready to write them down.

Part One: Real Christianity

What Jesus actually said. What he actually lived. Why it still matters.

1. The Carpenter's Rebellion

Why Jesus was a threat to the religious and political systems of his day.

2. Love Your Enemy, Not Just Your Neighbor

The most radical, most ignored command in all of Christianity.

3. You Cannot Serve Both God and Money

Jesus didn't just warn about wealth — he drew a line in the sand.

4. The Last Shall Be First

How Jesus flipped every social, political, and religious structure upside down.

5. He Sat With the Broken, Not the Powerful

Who Jesus chose to be near — and what that tells us about who belongs.

Part Two: Fake Christianity

The system that hijacked the message, weaponized the book, and silenced the truth.

1. The Sword and the Cross

How conquest was disguised as conversion — and what it cost the world.

2. Jesus Didn't Say Build an Empire

From movement to monarchy: when the Church became Caesar.

3. The Bible as a Weapon

Scripture used to justify slavery, war, sexism, and silence.

4. Salvation for Sale

How the Church got rich by monetizing guilt and fear.

5. God and Country

When Christianity became a political brand instead of a spiritual path.

6. The God of Shame

How sex was demonized while violence and control were protected.

7. Forgiveness Without Accountability

The weaponization of grace to shield abusers and silence victims.

8. How Faith Got Whitewashed

The colonized Jesus vs. the real one — and why it matters.

9. How Christianity Got Rich

From a barefoot rebel to billion-dollar institutions and golden altars.

10. The God of the Gaps

Why churches fear questions, curiosity, and spiritual growth.

11. The Fear Gospel

How hell replaced hope — and what it did to people's hearts.

Part Three: Reclaiming It

Finding truth in the ashes of religion.

1. If Jesus Walked Into Your Church Today

Would he stay? Would anyone recognize him?

2. The Message Is Still Good

How to keep what's real, and leave the rest behind.

3. Heaven on Earth

Letting Go of Religion to Find the Truth

Real Christianity - Chapter 1:
The Carpenter's Rebellion

Jesus wasn't executed because he told people to love each other.

He wasn't killed for healing the sick, feeding the hungry, or hanging out with prostitutes and tax collectors.

He was crucified — the most brutal public punishment the Roman Empire could dish out — because he disrupted the system. He threatened both religious authority and imperial power, and worst of all, he had a following.

This wasn't a soft-spoken guru preaching self-help tips under a fig tree. This was a man marching into temples, calling out corruption and hypocrisy, rebuking the elite, lifting up the poor, and preaching a version of "kingdom" that had nothing to do with emperors, armies, or thrones.

"The Kingdom of God is at Hand" — Not Caesar's

That phrase — "the kingdom of God" — sounds poetic now, but in his day, it was a loaded, dangerous idea. It was political language. A revolutionary phrase.

In Roman-occupied Judea, there was already a kingdom: Rome. There was already a king: Caesar. And Caesar wasn't just king — he was called "Son of God", "Savior of the World", and "Lord." All the titles that would later be given to Jesus? They were Caesar's first. So when Jesus said things like:

> "Give to Caesar what is Caesar's, and to God what is God's,"

> "Blessed are the poor,"

> "You cannot serve both God and money,"

> "The last shall be first,"

...he wasn't just making religious points. He was declaring a new world order, where the empire's values didn't apply. And that made him dangerous.

He Didn't Come With a Sword — And That Was the Threat

The Jews expected a messiah to overthrow Rome — to raise an army, claim the throne, and set their people free. But Jesus wasn't that kind of revolutionary.

He preached nonviolence, humility, and sacrifice. He said love your enemies. Pray for your persecutors. Don't hate the tax collector — invite him to dinner.

That's not how you win a war. That's how you win hearts. And the people in power knew that was even more dangerous.

He told people they didn't need priests to access God. He broke Sabbath laws to heal people. He said God cared more about mercy than rules.

And the religious leaders — the Pharisees, the temple elite — hated him for it.

Rome Didn't Misunderstand Him — They Understood Him Too Well

Crucifixion wasn't for common criminals. It was for insurrectionists. Rebels. Public threats.

Jesus was tried by the Roman governor, Pontius Pilate, and executed between two actual revolutionaries. The charge they nailed above his head read:

"Jesus of Nazareth, King of the Jews."

It was a mocking title. But also a warning:

"This is what we do to people who challenge Caesar."

They didn't kill him because he was misunderstood.

They killed him because they saw exactly what he was saying — and they couldn't control it.

From a Cross to a Crown

And here's where the twist begins.

The man who rejected power, rejected violence, rejected wealth — the man who literally washed feet and said "the greatest among you must be the servant of all" — would eventually be turned into a symbol of power, conquest, and empire.

The same empire that murdered him would eventually claim to follow him, build cathedrals in his name, and declare new Caesars as his representatives on Earth.

But we'll get to that.

This book is about the man they tried to silence, and why his message — if we actually listened to it — would still shake the world today.

Real Christianity - Chapter 2:
Love Your Enemy, Not Just Your Neighbor

If your version of Christianity includes loving your family and your friends but hating people on the other side of the political aisle — you're doing it wrong.

If your version of Christianity blesses soldiers going off to war, cheers when someone gets what they "deserve," or dehumanizes people for their race, religion, or identity — it's not Christianity.

Jesus said love your enemies.

Not tolerate them. Not pray that they wake up and become more like you. Not insult them on social media and say "I'll pray for you" with a side of sarcasm.

He said:

> "You have heard that it was said, 'Love your neighbor and hate your enemy.' But I tell you: Love your enemies and pray for those who persecute you, that you may be children of your Father in heaven."
>
> — Matthew 5:43–45

That's not a metaphor. That wasn't a parable. That was a command.

You Can't Weaponize That Message — So They Don't Preach It

Let's be honest: you almost never hear this verse from pulpits anymore. It's not marketable. It doesn't sell books or campaign signs. It's hard.

You can't build an army with it. You can't justify bombing a country with it. You can't demonize immigrants, atheists, gay people, or anyone else with it.

So they skip it.

But Jesus didn't skip it. He doubled down on it — over and over. He said turn the other cheek. He said don't resist an evildoer. He even forgave the men who nailed him to a cross.

Real Christianity is Anti-Vengeance

Let that sink in: the guy you say is your Lord and Savior died forgiving the people who were murdering him in real time.

That's not soft. That's not weak. That's next-level courage.

And it's everything modern fake Christianity runs from.

Because fake Christianity is built on fear and punishment. It needs enemies. It needs someone to blame, someone to burn, someone to point a finger at. Whether it's "the left," "the Muslims," "the atheists," or anyone that challenges the status quo.

Love That Makes No Sense

Here's the truth: Jesus' love didn't make sense then, and it doesn't make sense now.

He told stories where the hero was a foreigner (The Good Samaritan). He healed Roman soldiers' servants. He stopped his followers from using violence to defend him when he was arrested. He dined with the outcasts, not the elites.

He didn't say "go to church on Sunday." He said "feed the hungry, clothe the naked, visit the prisoner."

And when someone asked him "who is my neighbor?", looking for a loophole, Jesus basically said: "Everyone. Especially the people you hate."

It's Not Easy. That's the Point.

Real Christianity isn't supposed to be easy. It's not a club. It's not a brand. It's not a culture war.

It's choosing grace when revenge would feel better. It's showing compassion when judgment would be easier. It's staying tender when the world tells you to be tough and cold.

Jesus never said, "Be right."

He said, "Be love."

Real Christianity - Chapter 3:
You Cannot Serve Both God and Money

Jesus didn't hate money.

But he absolutely warned us about what it does to people.

He didn't say, "Try to balance both."

He said, you can't.

Point blank.

> *"No one can serve two masters. Either you will hate the one and love the other, or you will be devoted to the one and despise the other.*
>
> *You cannot serve both God and money."*
>
> — Matthew 6:24

That's not a metaphor. That's a line in the sand.

And yet… here we are, centuries later, with churches that preach Jesus while serving profit, luxury, and capitalism like it's holy.

Jesus Wasn't Subtle About Wealth

He said:

> *"Sell everything you own and give it to the poor."*
>
> *"Woe to you who are rich."*
>
> *"It's easier for a camel to go through the eye of a needle than for a rich man to enter the kingdom of God."*

He talked about money and power more than almost anything else — not because money is inherently evil, but because it competes with God for your loyalty.

It can shape your choices, your faith, your relationships, and your compassion — until it becomes your god.

And once it becomes your god, it's almost impossible to admit it.

Real Christianity Doesn't Worship Hustle

We live in a culture where success is measured by:
- How much you have
- How busy you are
- How many followers you've got

But Jesus wasn't building a brand. He was breaking chains.

He didn't say, "Grind harder." He said, "Consider the lilies."

He didn't say, "Buy land." He said, "Give it away."

He didn't say, "Blessed are the CEOs." He said, "Blessed are the poor."

Generosity Isn't Optional — It's Foundational

Jesus didn't suggest generosity — he demanded it.

In his kingdom:
- The rich give to the poor.
- The full share with the hungry.
- The safe shelter the vulnerable.

It wasn't charity. It was justice. And he called out religious people who tithed perfectly but ignored mercy, compassion, and equity.

If your version of Christianity protects your comfort but costs others their dignity — you're not following Jesus.

The Early Church Took It Seriously

In the book of Acts:

> *"All the believers were together and had everything in common. They sold property and possessions to give to anyone who had need."*
>
> — Acts 2:44–45

That wasn't communism. That was compassion.

It wasn't about a rule — **it was about a radical understanding that people matter more than property.**

The early Christians didn't build kingdoms.

They built community.

Today, Real Christians Still Live Like This

Not on TV. Not on stage. Not selling courses.

But in:

- Homeless shelters
- Soup kitchens
- Tiny apartments
- Grassroots movements
- Quiet lives of love

They're not chasing followers.

They're carrying crosses.

And they know that serving God means letting go of whatever makes you think you don't need him.

Money Isn't Evil — But It's Loud

It drowns out the Spirit.

It seduces your pride.

It makes you think you're in control.

Jesus said the truth would set you free — but money tries to buy the lie.

Real Christianity calls it out.

Fake Christianity tries to baptize it.

You can't do both.

Real Christianity - Chapter 4:
The Last Shall Be First

Jesus had a habit of flipping things upside down.

Not just tables in temples — but entire systems of value, status, and power.

He looked at a world obsessed with rich over poor, men over women, empire over citizen, holy over broken — and said:

> *"The last shall be first, and the first shall be last."*

— Matthew 20:16

I grew up hearing that verse, but no one really explained what it meant.

In church, they'd say it like it was a nice thought for the kids who didn't win the soccer game.

But Jesus wasn't talking about comfort.

He was talking about justice.

He was talking about flipping the script on a world that rewards power and punishes poverty.

And he wasn't subtle about it.

A Kingdom Built on Inversion

Everything Jesus said was backwards to the culture around him:

- He said the poor are blessed.

- He said the meek inherit the earth.
- He said the grieving will be comforted — not ignored.
- He said outsiders, not insiders, were often the ones closest to God.

It wasn't just comforting. It was dangerous.

Because he wasn't just trying to heal people — he was challenging the structure that put them at the bottom in the first place.

In the Empire, Hierarchy Rules — In the Kingdom, It's Broken

Rome was built like a pyramid:

- Caesar at the top
- The army just below
- Religious leaders right underneath
- And everyone else holding up the weight

And most churches today?

They still look like that. Pastors at the top. Volunteers at the bottom.

"Submit to authority." "Respect the chain of command."

"Touch not the Lord's anointed."

But Jesus didn't climb the ladder.

He kicked it over.

> "Whoever wants to be great among you must be your servant for even the Son of Man did not come to be served, but to serve."
>
> — Mark 10:43–45

You can't read that and still build a church around celebrity pastors in sneakers that cost more than your rent.

He Didn't Just Say It — He Lived It

He didn't hang out in palaces.

He ate with the rejected.

Touched the untouchable.

Defended the woman on the ground.

Told stories where the villain was the priest and the hero was the outcast.

He made the "least of these" his whole point.

So when he said "the last shall be first," he meant:
- The hungry are closer to heaven than the rich.
- The wounded are more honest than the righteous.
- The doubters and wanderers are welcome.
- The overlooked are seen.

This Isn't a Metaphor — It's a Warning

If you're always trying to be first —

If your church only lifts up the powerful —

If your version of faith rewards the loud, the wealthy, the polished —

You've missed the entire message.

Jesus was never about appearances.

He wasn't building an image.

He was building a revolution — and in his world, the least impressive people were the most important.

That doesn't sell books.

That doesn't build brands.

But it's real.

Why This Still Matters

Because some of the best people I know don't feel welcome in church.

They've been told they're wrong, broken, sinful, too loud, too quiet, too poor, too queer, too skeptical, too far gone.

But if Jesus meant what he said — they're exactly the kind of people he'd choose first.

And the ones doing the excluding? Might want to reread the part about who ends up first in line.

This Chapter Isn't About Religion. It's About Reality.

You don't need to believe in heaven to get the point here.

You don't need to be "saved" to recognize how upside-down the world is — and how healing it would be to flip it.

The last should be first.

The broken should be honored.

The forgotten should be lifted.

The arrogant should sit down.

And if Jesus was serious — we should all be rethinking who we admire, who we listen to, and who we're trying to be.

Real Christianity - Chapter 5:
He Sat With the Broken, Not the Powerful

If you've ever felt too far gone, too messy, too doubting, too weird, too anything —

you're probably the kind of person Jesus would've invited to dinner.

He didn't chase political leaders.

He didn't flatter priests.

He didn't schmooze kings.

He wasn't networking.

He sat with the wounded, the weird, the unacceptable, and the unwanted.

Not to fix them. Not to use them.

But because he actually liked them.

Who He Chose Tells You Everything

Look at his crew:
- Working class fishermen
- Tax collectors (traitors to their people)
- Zealots (political extremists)
- Prostitutes
- The sick, the outcast, the mentally ill
- Women (radical enough in that world)
- People with diseases no one would touch

He didn't just make room for them. He built his movement around them.

And that made people in power very, very uncomfortable.

Meanwhile, the "Holy" Got Called Out

The people with titles. The ones in robes.

The ones with influence and clout. They're the ones he dragged.

He called them:

"*Whitewashed tombs.*"

"*Clean on the outside, but full of rot inside.*"

— Matthew 23:27

He said:

"*You load people down with burdens, but won't lift a finger to help.*"

— Luke 11:46

He wasn't impressed by their knowledge. He wasn't moved by their status.

He saw through it — and he said so.

And Yet, Modern Churches Got It Backward

Now we celebrate:

- Mega pastors with branding teams
- Churches with VIP seating
- "Influencers for Jesus" with curated theology
- Sermons that never challenge anyone with power
- "Come as you are" slogans that really mean, "Clean it up fast"

We tell people to put on a smile. To stop asking questions.

To act holy before they're even healed.

Jesus never did that.

He Didn't Ask for a Resume. He Just Sat Down.

He didn't wait until people had it all together.

He didn't hand out purity checklists.

He didn't test theology before he offered grace.

He simply made space.

He made people feel seen — especially the ones the system had left behind.

And the people the world called unclean?

Those are the ones he called blessed.

If You've Been Told You're Not Welcome, Jesus Disagrees

If a church made you feel like a second-class soul —

if they told you you weren't good enough, holy enough, straight enough, clean enough —

Jesus would've disagreed with every word of it.

Because if he were here today,

he wouldn't be center stage in a stadium.

He'd be outside,

on the curb,

sitting with the ones who couldn't afford a ticket,

still calling them beloved.

Fake Christianity - Chapter 1:
The Sword and the Cross

If Jesus preached love, why did so many people die in his name?

Why did Indigenous children get stolen from their families to be "civilized" in church-run schools?

Why did millions of Africans get shackled, branded, and sold into slavery — while their captors held Bibles in their hands?

Why did missionaries roll into nations with crosses in one hand and guns or opium in the other?

The answer is simple and horrifying:

because power found a way to hijack the message.

It took the man who said "love your enemy" and turned him into a mascot for conquest.

This isn't Christianity. It's Fake Christianity — a system dressed in robes, quoting scripture, smiling from pulpits… while marching lockstep with empire, colonizers, and war.

Jesus Didn't Colonize — Empires Did

The Jesus of the Gospels never forced anyone to follow him.

He didn't convert by threat.

He didn't baptize with bayonets.

He didn't ride with armies.

He washed feet.

But fast-forward a few hundred years, and his name is stamped on everything from crusade banners to slave ships to concentration camp gates.

How?

Because once the Roman Empire adopted Christianity, they changed the mission:

From "Serve the least of these" to "Conquer in the name of the Lord."

The Cross Goes Global — But Not in the Way Jesus Meant

In the Americas:

- European missionaries followed conquistadors.
- Crosses were planted in the soil right after the flags.
- Natives were forced to convert, abandon their languages, and abandon their cultures.
- Those who resisted? Killed. Those who obeyed? Often died anyway — from disease, starvation, or forced labor.

Estimated Indigenous deaths across the Americas post-contact?

Over 50 million. And much of it happened with Christian approval — or at least Christian silence.

In China:

- Christian missionaries arrived under the pretense of spreading the Gospel.
- Meanwhile, Western governments were flooding China with opium, decimating families and cultures.
- The result? Addiction, humiliation, war, and the death of millions — all while preaching "salvation."

In Africa:

- Missionaries preached submission while colonizers took land and bodies.
- Churches justified slavery using twisted Bible verses.
- Whole populations were "converted" at the end of a whip.

This wasn't faith. This was spiritual colonization.

What Would Jesus Say?

He might say:

> "You traveled over land and sea to win a single convert, and when you have succeeded, you make them twice as much a child of hell as you are."

— Matthew 23:15

That wasn't a quote aimed at pagans. That was Jesus talking to religious leaders who turned their faith into a tool for control.

Sound familiar?

The Real Poison: Holy Justification

The violence was horrific — but maybe the worst part was the moral righteousness that came with it.

"We're saving their souls."

"We're civilizing them."

"We're bringing them the truth."

That's how fake Christianity works: it commits harm while convincing itself it's doing good.

That's how you get churches with slave-owning pastors.

That's how you get "Christian nations" committing genocide.

That's how you get evil with a phony halo on top.

Fake Christianity - Chapter 2:
Jesus Didn't Say Build an Empire

Jesus didn't build a church.

He didn't fundraise for a building.

He didn't write laws.

He didn't run for office.

He didn't pick up a sword.

He didn't even own a home.

The Jesus of history wandered from village to village without a title, a temple, or a throne, teaching people to care less about power and more about people.

He talked about serving, not ruling.

Dying to self, not climbing a ladder.

He said the last would be first, and the first would be last.

He said to give without expecting anything in return.

He said don't store up treasures — especially not on earth.

So how did we end up with palaces, gold crosses, televised mega-sermons, popes with armies, and churches in bed with politics?

The answer? Somewhere along the way, the church stopped following Jesus… and started imitating Caesar.

The Roman Makeover of Christianity

It started with Emperor Constantine in the early 4th century.

Before him, Christians were:

- Underground.
- Persecuted.

- Poor.
- Radical.
- Sharing resources, refusing to kill, feeding the hungry, loving enemies.

After Constantine, Christianity gradually became:
- Legalized.
- Institutionalized.
- Funded by the state.
- Militarized.
- Structured like an imperial bureaucracy.

The Council of Nicaea (325 CE) was the first big step in codifying doctrine, silencing dissent, and deciding who counted as "Christian." It wasn't about love anymore. It was about control.

And once Rome was in, it was game on.

The church merged with empire, and for the next thousand years, it would act more like a kingdom than a faith.

Holy Roman Empire, Unholy Agenda

Under the banner of Christ, empires:
- Crowned kings and waged wars.
- Burned heretics.
- Silenced scientists.
- Took land, gold, and lives.
- Taxed the poor while living in luxury.

Popes became political figures. Bishops controlled territory. The church owned massive amounts of land and became one of the wealthiest institutions in human history — all while quoting a man who said "give it all away."

Christianity stopped being a message and became a machine.

From a Movement to a Monument

The early followers of Jesus were called The Way — not "Christians." It was about a way of life, not a membership.

They shared food. They refused to fight. They welcomed outsiders.

They had no buildings.

No cathedrals.

No celebrity pastors.

But once fake Christianity took hold, the church became obsessed with structures — literal and symbolic:

- Buildings bigger than the poor neighborhoods around them.
- Hierarchies that placed men over women, clergy over laity, Europeans over everyone else.
- Doctrines that elevated compliance over compassion.

Jesus Said, "Go" — Not "Conquer"

The Great Commission — "Go and make disciples of all nations" — has been twisted into a colonizer's mission statement.

But Jesus didn't say "force."

He didn't say "invade."

He didn't say "rule."

He said go, teach, baptize, love, serve.

The message was always invitation, never imposition.

Always example, never enforcement.

But fake Christianity turned it into conquest.

Ask Yourself: Is My Church a Movement or a Monument?

Does it lift up the poor — or lecture them?

Does it challenge power — or benefit from it?

Does it look like Jesus — or just say it does?

If the walls are taller than the arms are open, you're not in a church.

You're in an empire with a steeple.

Fake Christianity - Chapter 3:
The Bible as a Weapon

Jesus said, "The truth will set you free."

But for centuries, people have used the Bible to chain others down.

They quoted scripture while justifying slavery, launching wars, oppressing women, erasing cultures, and silencing dissent.

And not just fringe groups — governments, monarchs, and entire denominations built systems of control using verses as ammunition.

This chapter isn't about whether the Bible is good or bad. It's about how Fake Christianity cherry-picked the parts that served the powerful, and buried the rest.

Slavery in Jesus's Name

Let's start with the ugliest truth:

The transatlantic slave trade was backed by Bibles.

Enslavers quoted:

"Slaves, obey your earthly masters with respect and fear."

— Ephesians 6:5

"Cursed be Canaan! The lowest of slaves will he be to his brothers."

— Genesis 9:25

The second verse was weaponized to claim that Black people were "cursed" and destined for slavery — a racist distortion that fueled centuries of oppression.

Pastors preached it. Politicians defended it.

And slave ships had names like The Good Ship Jesus.

Never mind that Jesus never owned slaves.

Never mind that he said love your neighbor as yourself.

Never mind that the early Christian communities shared everything and erased social divisions.

They found a few verses and used them to justify generations of trauma.

The Crusades: Holy War, Unholy Intentions

Starting in 1095, Christian Europe launched hundreds of years of religious wars, invading the Middle East under the banner of the cross.

Preachers promised forgiveness of sins in exchange for violence. Soldiers marched with crosses on their armor, convinced they were doing God's work by massacring Muslims, Jews, and even other Christians.

Jesus said:

> *"Put your sword back in its place... all who draw the sword will die by the sword."*

— Matthew 26:52

But Fake Christianity said:

"Take the sword. God is on our side."

The Bible was now a license to kill — as long as you had the right banner.

Silencing Women, Elevating Men

Jesus consistently elevated women — talking with them, learning from them, and appearing to women first after his resurrection.

But that didn't stop church leaders from quoting:

> *"I do not permit a woman to teach or to assume authority over a man; she must be quiet."*

— 1 Timothy 2:12

Used out of context and wielded with certainty, this one verse did centuries of damage:

- Women were banned from leadership.
- Called inferior.
- Blamed for sin ("Eve's fault").
- And kept silent while men built kingdoms in Jesus's name.

Fake Christianity weaponized patriarchy and called it holy.

Conversion by Force

The Bible says:

"Go and make disciples of all nations..."

— Matthew 28:19

That was supposed to mean go love, go serve, go teach.

But Fake Christianity read it as go conquer.

In Latin America, Asia, and Africa, this became the mission statement for forced conversions, cultural genocide, and ethnic cleansing — all stamped with scripture.

The real Jesus offered a hand.

Fake Christianity delivered ultimatums.

Why This Matters Today

Because it's still happening.

You've got politicians using Bible verses to:

- Block immigrants.
- Control women's bodies.
- Defund the poor.

- Justify military aggression.

You've got preachers using scripture to:

- Shame gay people.
- Amass wealth.
- Silence questions.
- Push conspiracy theories.

They quote verses.

They skip the context.

And they ignore the red letters.

Scripture Without Spirit is Just Ammunition

The Bible is powerful. It has inspired freedom movements, civil rights leaders, and acts of courage and compassion around the world.

But in the hands of empire?

It becomes a weapon.

And Fake Christianity has been locked and loaded for centuries.

Fake Christianity - Chapter 4:
Salvation for Sale

Jesus flipped the tables when he saw people selling salvation in the temple.

If he walked into a modern church today — the kind with ATMs in the lobby, $10,000 suits in the pulpit, and donation links every ten seconds — he might flip a few more.

Because somewhere along the way, the message of "Come, all who are weary" became "Pay up, or burn forever."

From Grace to Transaction

The early Jesus movement was built on freely given grace.

- You didn't need to buy access.
- You didn't need to climb a ladder.
- You didn't need to tithe 10% to a CEO in robes.

You needed a heart that was open, not a wallet that was full.

But as the Church grew into an institution — with political power, land, armies, and influence — it needed more than just converts.

It needed income.

And fear is very profitable.

Indulgences: The Original Pay-to-Pray

In the Middle Ages, the Catholic Church sold indulgences — literal pieces of paper claiming to reduce your time in purgatory.

Not only could you buy your own forgiveness, you could even prepay for sins or purchase redemption for your dead relatives.

They told the poor: "Give what you have, and maybe God will go easy on you."

This system bankrolled palaces, art, wars, and entire empires — all while quoting a man who said, "Blessed are the poor."

Martin Luther Nailed It — Literally

In 1517, a German monk named Martin Luther had had enough. He wrote 95 theses calling out the Church's corruption — especially the selling of salvation — and nailed them to the church door.

This moment sparked the Protestant Reformation, a rebellion against spiritual manipulation.

But the spirit of the hustle?

It didn't die. It just got rebranded.

Enter the Mega-Church

Fast forward to today. Now it's not indulgences — it's "seed faith."

Give more, get blessed.

> "Plant a $1,000 seed and watch your financial breakthrough come."

> "God wants you to be rich, and if you're not, you're doing it wrong."

These pastors fly private.

They preach prosperity.

They take from the struggling to build empires in Jesus's name.

Meanwhile, Jesus said:

> "Do not store up for yourselves treasures on earth..."

— Matthew 6:19

And:

> "You cannot serve both God and money."

— Matthew 6:24

But fake Christianity doesn't quote those verses.

It skips them.

Deletes them.

Spins them into something more marketable.

Fear Sells. So They Sell Fear.

For centuries, churches have told people:
- You're born broken.
- God is angry.
- Hell is coming.
- And only we can save you.

They call it love, but it's often emotional blackmail dressed up in religious language.

That's not grace.

That's spiritual capitalism.

Grace Was Never for Sale

You don't earn love.

You don't buy redemption.

You don't swipe your card to be worthy.

If Jesus is the example, then everything that's being sold in his name — miracles, blessings, forgiveness — is already free.

The price was never yours to pay.

But Fake Christianity?

It put up a paywall anyway.

Fake Christianity - Chapter 5:
God and Country

Jesus never said, "Blessed are the powerful."

He never said, "Worship your nation."

He never told anyone to pledge allegiance to an empire, carry a weapon, or put their trust in a flag.

And yet, all over the world — especially in the United States — Christianity has been twisted into a nationalist religion, where loving your country is treated as equivalent to loving God… and questioning your country is seen as heresy.

This is Fake Christianity at it's most dangerous — not just selling out the message, but welding it to power.

The Flag in the Pulpit

Step into some churches today, and you'll see:

- A Bible on one side of the altar, a flag on the other.
- Songs praising God and America in the same verse.
- Sermons telling you that "real" Christians vote a certain way, live a certain way, and look a certain way.

That's not the gospel.

That's propaganda.

Jesus Wasn't a Patriot

Let's get this straight:

- Jesus lived in a military-occupied country.
- He rejected the political expectations of his time.
- People wanted him to be a national liberator, but he said "my kingdom is not of this world."

When they tried to crown him king, he walked away.

When pressed about taxes, he turned the question inside out.

When he was crucified, he forgave both the soldiers and the crowd.

He didn't take sides. He took a stand —

for love, mercy, and truth, no matter where it led.

The Rise of National Christianity

Fake Christianity took that universal, counter-cultural message…

And turned it into a tool for empire building.

In Europe:

Kings claimed divine right — saying God chose them to rule.

Churches blessed conquests, crusades, and colonization.

To challenge the king was to challenge God.

In America:

Faith was sewn into national identity — "In God We Trust," "One Nation Under God."

But whose God?

- The one who said "love your enemies"?
- Or the one who gets invoked when we're dropping bombs?

The American version of Christianity has too often been used to:

- Justify slavery.
- Erase Indigenous peoples.
- Ban immigrants and refugees.
- Elevate one race, one class, one worldview.

All while calling itself holy.

Christian Nationalism Isn't Christianity

Christianity says:

> "There is no Jew or Gentile, slave or free, male or female — you are all one in Christ."

> — Galatians 3:28

Fake Christianity says:

> "There's us — and there's them. We're right, they're wrong. We're chosen, they're condemned."

Christianity says:

> "Welcome the stranger."

> "Feed the hungry."

> "Do justice."

> "Walk humbly."

Fake Christianity builds border walls and then prays in front of them.

When Churches Become Campaign Stops

In modern politics, Christianity is often used like a brand sponsor.

Politicians:
- Quote a verse or two. (or not)
- Pose with a Bible.
- Say "God bless America."
- And suddenly they get a free pass from people who claim to follow the same Jesus who called out this very hypocrisy and corruption.

Pastors:
- Use their pulpits to push party lines.
- Shame people for voting "wrong."
- Turn congregations into voting blocs, not spiritual communities.

The message gets drowned in ideology.

The cross gets draped in red, white, and blue.

And Jesus?

He becomes a campaign prop.

There Is No Christian Nation — Only Christian People

Jesus didn't come to build a government.

He came to transform hearts.

The moment churches forgot that, they stopped being churches and became political action committees.

Faith Doesn't Need a Flag

If your church is more concerned with elections than compassion,

more devoted to policies than people,

and more loyal to politicians than to Christ…

…you're not in a church.

You're in a rally.

And Jesus left the building a long time ago.

Fake Christianity - Chapter 6:
The God of Shame

If you grew up in a church, you probably heard a lot about sex.

Don't have it.

Don't think about it.

Don't wear that.

Don't be that.

But you probably didn't hear nearly as much about:
- Greed
- Power
- Systemic violence
- Or Jesus' actual teachings on love, mercy, and economic justice

Fake Christianity became a system that shamed bodies while protecting brutality — a purity-obsessed culture that taught kids to fear sex more than war, hell more than hate.

This chapter is about that warped imbalance.

And how it never came from Jesus.

Jesus Didn't Police Bodies — He Freed Them

Jesus never shamed a woman for her sexuality.

In fact, the people religious leaders wanted to stone or exclude, Jesus lifted up, defended, and honored.

- The "sinful woman" who washed his feet with her tears? He defended her.

- The woman caught in adultery? He said, "Let the one without sin cast the first stone."

- The Samaritan woman at the well — married five times and living with a man? Jesus spoke with her respectfully, taught her, and revealed his identity to her. She became the first evangelist in John's Gospel.

Jesus never reduced anyone to their past.

He never used shame as a weapon.

So how did shame become the church's favorite tool?

The Purity Obsession

Starting especially in the 4th–5th centuries, church fathers like Augustine brought their own baggage into theology — teaching that sex was inherently dirty, women were temptresses, and the body was something to be subdued.

This evolved into centuries of:

- Virgin worship.
- Women blamed for men's lust.
- Clothing rules.
- Celibacy treated as holier than love.
- Sex education replaced with fear and silence.

And all of it wrapped in guilt, shame, and eternal consequences.

Meanwhile — the same churches that preached purity were often:

- Protecting abusers behind closed doors.
- Silencing victims.
- Ignoring justice.

Policing Sex, Ignoring Violence

Let's be real: churches that tell women not to show skin or boys not to masturbate rarely preach with the same fire about:

- Racism
- Mass incarceration
- Corrupt politicians
- Greedy corporations
- Domestic violence
- Child abuse scandals within the church itself

Why? Because sex is easy to control.

It's internal.

Personal.

You can trap people in fear of their own minds.

But standing up against systemic sin?

That takes courage.

It risks funding.

It might challenge the very people sitting in the front row writing checks.

So Fake Christianity stays quiet on the hard stuff — and loud on the easy targets.

It's Not About Holiness. It's About Control.

Real Christianity invites people into transformation — rooted in love, trust, and mutual respect.

Fake Christianity builds rules and fences:

- Who can love who.
- Who's welcome at the table.
- Who's "clean" and who's "unclean."

And it does all this while ignoring the rot in its own heart.

Jesus Broke the Shame Cycle

He didn't say:

> "You're dirty and broken."

He said:

> "You're loved. Go in peace. Leave behind what hurts you — not because you're worthless, but because you're already worthy."

That's not shame.

That's freedom.

What the Church Should Have Said

Instead of "don't touch yourself or God will cry," they should have said:

"You are not your urges. You are not your shame. You are not your worst thought."

Instead of "God hates gay people," they should have said:

"God loves every person with breath in their lungs and a heart in their chest."

Instead of turning sex into sin, they should have taught about respect, consent, vulnerability, love, and sacred connection.

Instead of shame, they should have offered healing.

Shame Is a Bad Teacher

Jesus taught with truth, grace, and presence.

Fake Christianity teaches with fear, silence, and punishment.

That's not holiness. That's manipulation.

And it's time we call it what it is — and break the cycle.

Fake Christianity - Chapter 7:
Forgiveness Without Accountability

Jesus taught forgiveness.

But he never meant "shut up and move on."

He didn't mean "forgive and forget while the person who hurt you stays in power."

He didn't mean "stay silent so the church looks clean on the outside."

But for far too long, fake Christianity has used forgiveness as a weapon — not for healing, but for hiding. Especially when the abuser is someone important.

A pastor. A parent. A leader. A donor.

The Cycle of Abuse, the Shield of Grace

It goes like this:

- Someone in power causes harm.
- The victim comes forward.
- The church preaches "grace" and "reconciliation."
- The abuser "repents" — often in public, with tears.
- The church rallies around them. "None of us are perfect."
- The victim? Forgotten. Or worse — blamed for "division."

This isn't forgiveness.

It's emotional laundering.

When "Forgiveness" Is Just Damage Control

Churches often say:

> "Don't gossip. Don't judge. Forgive and move on."

But what they really mean is:

> "Don't disrupt the system. Don't embarrass us. Don't make it messy."

And who benefits from that silence? Abusers. Predators. Manipulators.

People who learned they can sin as long as they cry and quote a few verses after.

Jesus Didn't Protect the Powerful — He Protected the Vulnerable

He never excused abuse.

He never told the hurting to "move on."

He never covered for religious leaders who exploited people.

He said things like:

> "Woe to you… you clean the outside of the cup, but inside you are full of greed and self-indulgence."
>
> — Matthew 23:25

He didn't stay silent when they turned the temple into a business.

He stood in front of a crowd with stones and said: "Not today."

If someone abused their power, Jesus called them out. Not covered them up.

Accountability Is Not Cancel Culture — It's Repentance

Real repentance isn't just saying sorry. It's:

- Stepping down from power.
- Making things right.
- Listening to the people you hurt.

- Accepting consequences.

Fake Christianity loves cheap grace — the kind that lets leaders stay in charge, reputations stay clean, and wounds stay hidden.

But real grace?

It requires truth.

And truth doesn't come with a PR strategy.

When the Church Sides with Abusers, It Stops Being Church

If your church protects the predator but silences the victim —

That's not faith.

That's corruption.

If your pastor preaches redemption but never once says the words "I believe you" to a survivor —

That's not grace.

That's rot.

If your community only offers comfort to the person who caused the harm —

That's not Jesus.

That's Caesar in mitre.

Healing Needs Justice, Not Just Prayers

You can't heal from a wound that someone else keeps denying.

You can't forgive what you're not allowed to speak out loud.

And you shouldn't have to.

Not in the name of "unity."

Not to keep the tithes flowing.

Not to protect the brand.

Forgiveness is beautiful. But without accountability, it's a lie.

And fake Christianity has been lying for a long time.

Fake Christianity - Chapter 8:
How Faith Got Whitewashed

Jesus wasn't white.

He wasn't blonde.

He wasn't blue-eyed.

He didn't speak English.

He wasn't American.

He wasn't safe.

He was a brown-skinned, Middle Eastern Jew born under occupation — a man who lived in an oppressed region, spoke Aramaic, was probably homeless, and challenged the religious and political authorities of his time until they executed him in public.

But somehow, over the centuries, that radical peasant was transformed into a European-looking savior draped in empire — a Jesus who looked more like his oppressors than himself.

This chapter is about how that happened — and why it still matters.

Step One: Erase His Color

From the 4th century onward, as Christianity was absorbed by the Roman Empire, the image of Jesus began to change. He went from a poor brown man with calloused hands to a pale, regal, robed icon, more king than carpenter.

Renaissance artists — mostly white, mostly European — painted him in their own image. Not out of malice, maybe, but out of control.

Because as Christianity became a tool of European power, it couldn't have a savior who looked like the people being colonized. It needed a white Jesus. A safe Jesus. A Jesus who blessed the people in charge — not the ones they were enslaving.

Step Two: Use That Image to Conquer the World

When European powers set out to colonize the globe, they brought three things:

- Flags
- Guns
- And crosses

Missionaries told Indigenous people:

"*We come to bring you salvation.*"

But behind that promise was:

- Forced conversions
- Suppression of language and culture
- Theft of land and identity
- Disease, death, and domination — all wrapped in "God's will"

In Africa, Asia, and the Americas, a white Jesus was used to convince millions that their traditions were evil, their gods were false, and their salvation could only come from the same people taking everything from them.

That's not faith.

That's religious colonization.

Christianity Was Never Meant to Be White

The early church was full of diversity:

- Jews
- Greeks
- Egyptians
- Ethiopians
- Syrians

The Bible itself mentions:

- Simon of Cyrene, a Black man from Africa, who helped carry Jesus's cross.
- The church in Antioch, where followers were first called "Christians," was multiethnic.
- The Ethiopian eunuch, one of the first non-Jewish converts.

But as time went on, whitewashed theology replaced history. European dominance became "God's plan." And whiteness became entangled with holiness — a lie that continues to damage lives today.

Slavery, Supremacy, and the God Card

In the U.S., white Christian leaders:

- Used the Bible to justify slavery.
- Built seminaries that trained pro-slavery pastors.
- Preached obedience to masters, while branding human beings as property.

Even after slavery ended, white churches largely:

- Opposed civil rights.
- Resisted integration.
- Sat silently through lynchings and segregation.

Why? Because the version of Christianity they followed wasn't built on the teachings of Jesus — it was built on power, preservation, and the myth of racial superiority.

Modern Christianity Still Feels the Effects

Walk into most churches in America and Jesus is still white.

The pastors are still white.

The congregation is still segregated.

And the theology often centers on European interpretations of scripture as if they are universal.

Meanwhile, voices from the global south, from Black theology, from Indigenous spirituality — are ignored, dismissed, or silenced.

That's not an accident. That's a legacy.

What Whitewashing Stole From Everyone

It didn't just steal truth from people of color —

it stole the revolutionary power of Jesus from everyone.

Because if you can make Jesus look like the empire,

You can make obedience look like faith.

You can make silence look like holiness.

You can make injustice look like God's plan.

Jesus Was Brown, Poor, Oppressed, and Unafraid

If your version of Christianity can't handle that,

You're not following Jesus.

You're following a marketing campaign.

And the kingdom he talked about?

It was never white.

It was never Western.

It was never about building altars on stolen land.

Missionaries told Indigenous people:

"We come to bring you salvation."

But behind that salvation came slavery, land theft, forced conversion, stolen languages, and genocide — all backed by a whitewashed image of Jesus that looked more like the colonizer than the Christ.

The real Jesus — the brown-skinned Jewish man who challenged empire — would have been killed by the same people waving those crosses. And yet, they claimed his name while crushing the very people he said he came to defend.

Christianity Became the Cover for White Supremacy

Let's be clear:

- The slave trade was blessed by Christian leaders.
- Jim Crow laws were supported by pastors quoting scripture.
- Indigenous genocide was carried out by Christian governments and "mission" efforts.
- And even now, in churches across the Western world, whiteness is still treated as default, as holy, as "chosen."

It's not just the stained-glass windows showing a European Jesus.

It's the sermons that ignore racial injustice.

It's the churches that stay silent during police killings but scream about property damage.

It's the institutions that quote MLK once a year but would've called him divisive when he was alive.

Jesus Was Never on the Side of the Powerful

He said:

"Whatever you did for the least of these, you did for me."

— Matthew 25:40

He said:

"Woe to you who are rich, for you have already received your comfort."

— Luke 6:24

He never blessed empire. He never endorsed domination.

And he damn sure didn't look like a Renaissance king in a marble palace.

Why It Still Matters Today

Because if the image of Jesus is whitewashed,

then the message of Jesus gets whitewashed too.

Suddenly:

- Justice becomes "radical."
- Equality becomes "political."
- Empathy becomes "soft."
- And the faith of a brown-skinned rebel gets turned into a weapon to protect the status quo.

That's Fake Christianity — where Jesus is used to preserve comfort, not to challenge cruelty.

The Real Jesus Was Dangerous to Empire

And he still is — if you're willing to see him.

He stood with the marginalized.

He ate with the rejected.

He preached liberation.

He was killed by the system, not lifted by it.

You don't need a blonde Jesus.

You don't need a nationalist Jesus.

You don't need a colonizer Jesus.

You need the real one — even if he makes you uncomfortable.

Especially if he does.

Fake Christianity - Chapter 9:
How Christianity Got Rich

Jesus said,

> "Foxes have dens and birds have nests, but the Son of Man has no place to lay his head."

— Luke 9:58

He was broke. Homeless. Dependent on the hospitality of strangers.

He told his followers to leave their possessions, give to the poor, and trust God — not wealth — to sustain them.

So how did we go from a carpenter with no shoes to cathedrals made of gold, popes in palaces, and pastors flying private jets?

The answer? Somewhere along the line, the church stopped following Jesus and started chasing power.

The Early Church Was Broke — On Purpose

In the first couple hundred years after Jesus, the church had no money and no influence. And that was by design.

Early Christians:
- Shared their resources.
- Cared for the sick and dying when no one else would.
- Refused to participate in war.
- Lived simply and sacrificially.

They were often persecuted by the rich — not endorsed by them.

But as the empire began to fall apart, it needed a new source of authority. And the church? It had loyalty. It had structure. It had reach. So the deal was made:

"You get protection. We get power."

Constantine's Conversion: The Turning Point

In 313 CE, Emperor Constantine legalized Christianity. By 380 CE, Theodosius made it the official state religion of Rome.

And suddenly:

- The church had state funding.
- Bishops had political influence.
- Church leaders were no longer rebels — they were administrators.

The teachings of Jesus got institutionalized. Then monetized. Then weaponized.

From Movement to Empire

Over the next thousand years, the church amassed:

- Land
- Taxes
- Treasuries
- Political clout

It became a feudal power, with popes who ruled like kings and bishops who lived like nobility.

Meanwhile, Jesus had said:

> *"Do not store up treasures on earth... you cannot serve both God and money."*

— Matthew 6:19, 24

But Fake Christianity heard:

"Store everything. Own everything. Bless the rich and ignore the poor."

The Vatican: A Kingdom in Disguise

Let's talk real numbers:

- The Vatican is its own sovereign state, with its own bank, property empire, and priceless art collection.
- Its net worth is estimated in the billions, though the true total is hard to calculate.
- And yet, it often refuses to release full records on sexual abuse payouts, financial scandals, and more.

It looks a lot more like Rome than Galilee.

And it's not just the Catholic Church.

Evangelical megachurches rake in millions. Televangelists sell prosperity while hoarding jets, mansions, and book deals.

All while people in their congregations struggle to buy groceries.

Tithes, Guilt, and the Church ATM

In many churches, you're told:

- "God wants 10%."
- "If you don't give, you're robbing God."
- "Your blessing is tied to your sacrifice."

But where does that money go?

Sometimes:

- To bloated salaries.
- To stage lights and fog machines.
- To debt on buildings too big to clean.

Rarely:
- To feed the poor.
- To shelter the unhoused.
- To liberate the oppressed.

Jesus told a rich man:

"Sell everything you own, give it to the poor, and follow me."

— Matthew 19:21

Fake Christianity tells the poor:

"Give everything to us, and God might bless you later."

The Church Got Rich While the World Stayed Poor

Jesus didn't stay silent when the temple turned into a marketplace.

Today, the church just adds a donation link and calls it ministry.

If Jesus came back today, he wouldn't need to cleanse the temple.

He'd need to cleanse the un-taxed "nonprofit" industrial complex in his name.

In 2018 a "preacher" who already owned a private jet told his congregation that God wanted him to have a second. Why? Because the first jet couldn't make it all the way around the world without refueling. He said God told him flying commercial was like "getting in a long tube with a bunch of demons."

And they bought it. Literally. The church raised the 54 million dollars.

That's not ministry. That's malpractice.

Real Christianity Lifts the Poor — Fake Christianity Just Profits Off Them

It's time to ask:

- Does your church have a missions budget bigger than its benevolence fund?
- Does it spend more on marketing than it gives away?
- Do its leaders live more like Caesar than Christ?

Because if so…

That's not the church.

That's a business.

Fake Christianity, Chapter 10:
The God of the Gaps

When I started asking questions, I didn't do it to be rebellious.

I wasn't trying to tear anything down.

I was just curious.

Why did God need blood to forgive people?

Why are there so many contradictions in the Bible?

Why are some churches more obsessed with being right than being kind?

Why does this feel more like a social club than a spiritual place?

Why is Jesus barely mentioned — unless it's to back up a message about giving money or voting right?

And most of all:

Why does asking feel like betrayal?

Churches Teach Faith — But Punish Thought

In a lot of places, Christianity teaches people to:

- Obey authority.
- Trust doctrine.
- Never question the Bible.
- Accept things that don't make sense — or else.

You're told:

"Lean not on your own understanding."

"God's ways are higher than ours."

"Doubt is the devil's voice."

But here's the thing: Jesus never rebuked honest doubt.

He rebuked hypocrisy, greed, and self-righteousness — not people trying to figure things out.

The God of the Gaps

There's a phrase some theologians use: "God of the gaps."

It means filling every hole in knowledge with "God did it."

Can't explain something? God.

Don't understand suffering? God.

Science doesn't have an answer yet? God.

That's not faith. That's fear of uncertainty.

And when religion is built on that kind of fear, it starts to collapse when people ask real questions.

So the solution becomes:

Keep people from asking.

Doubt Isn't the Opposite of Faith — It's the Start of It

Doubt is what makes faith real.

Otherwise, you're just parroting what you were taught.

Jesus didn't shame Thomas for needing proof.

He showed up.

He said, "Touch my wounds."

He didn't say, "Get out of the room for questioning me."

He met him where he was — with evidence and compassion.

Imagine if more churches responded like that.

Why So Many People Leave

It's not because they're lazy.

Or sinful.

Or want to party.

Or "fell into the world."

A lot of people walk away from church because:

- They were curious and got shut down.
- They were hurting and got shamed.
- They were thinking and got called rebellious.
- They saw how business-like it all felt.
- They were searching for truth and found manipulation, marketing, and fear.

They didn't walk away from Jesus.

They walked away from a system that doesn't trust people to think for themselves.

Curiosity Is a Gift — Not a Sin

If your faith can't survive a question,

It's not faith.

It's control.

If your church avoids difficult conversations,

It's not protecting truth.

It's protecting its structure.

And if your theology requires shutting people up,

You're not doing God's work.

You're building a cult.

Jesus Didn't Come to Create Followers — He Came to Create Seekers

He taught in stories — not formulas.

He asked questions more than he gave answers.

He praised children for their wonder, and called out adults for their arrogance.

Real faith isn't scared of being wrong.

Real faith can sit with mystery.

Real faith says: "I don't know… but I want to find out."

That's not weakness. That's wisdom.

Fake Christianity, Chapter 11:
The Fear Gospel

If your faith is built on fear, it's not faith — it's manipulation.

If the main reason you believe in God is just in case hell is real,

you're not being led — you're being controlled.

And if you've ever been told that the only way God will love you is if you follow the rules, give money, show up every week, and never screw up — you've been handed a weaponized version of faith.

This chapter is about that version.

The one where love is conditional,

and fear is the glue.

The Original Message Was Hope

Jesus didn't walk around threatening people with hell.

He walked around healing, feeding, forgiving, and welcoming.

He spent most of his time lifting people up, not scaring them into submission.

He didn't use fear to sell God.

He used compassion to show who God already was.

He didn't say, "Get your act together or you're done."

He said, "Come to me, all who are weary."

And yet somewhere along the way, we flipped it.

Because Fear Works — and the Church Knew It

It's simple:

- Tell people they're going to hell.
- Tell them there's only one way out.
- Sell them the solution.
- Repeat until wealthy.

Fear became the hook.

Heaven became the prize.

Hell became the motivation.

And suddenly, Christianity wasn't about love, grace, or liberation.

It was about survival.

Hell Became the Centerpiece

Let's be real:

The modern idea of hell — fiery torture forever — isn't even in the Bible the way people think it is.

- The Hebrew Bible barely talks about it.
- Jesus used the word Gehenna — which was an actual burning garbage pit outside Jerusalem, not a spiritual dimension.
- "Eternal conscious torment" wasn't a universal Christian belief until long after Jesus was gone.

But it sells. And once you convince people they're already damned,

you can convince them to do just about anything to get out of it.

The Business of Fear

Fake Christianity became a fear economy.

- "You're sinful by nature."
- "God is holy and angry."
- "You need to be covered in Jesus' blood to be acceptable."
- "One wrong move and you're done."

Fear keeps the seats filled.

It keeps the donations flowing.

It keeps people obedient.

But it doesn't heal.

It doesn't build character.

It doesn't teach love.

It teaches shame.

Let's Be Clear: Shame Is Not a Spiritual Tool

If your church uses fear to keep you in line,

that's not faith — that's control.

If your pastor tells you you're broken beyond repair — but lucky because they have the cure — that's a scam.

If your belief system says God loves you, but only if you're good, pure, holy, and tithed up — that's not Jesus. That's a vending machine with a pulpit.

Jesus didn't say "be afraid."

He said "be free."

Jesus Didn't Dangle Hell Over People — He Sat With Them

He didn't show up screaming about flames.

He showed up with food.

He touched people no one would touch.

He healed what was broken.

He restored dignity.

He said "You're forgiven" — before they even asked for it.

And when he talked about judgment,

he wasn't talking about individuals who cussed or skipped church.

He was talking about systems.

Corrupt leaders.

Religious hypocrisy.

Hell wasn't the centerpiece.

Love was.

If You Were Scared Into Believing, It's Okay to Start Over

You're not weak for asking questions.

You're not backsliding for healing from fear.

You're not a "lukewarm Christian" for wanting a better reason to believe than "or else."

You're allowed to grow out of fear-based faith.

You're allowed to find something deeper, more honest, and more human.

Because If God Is Love…

…then the fear gospel isn't just wrong — it's blasphemous.

Perfect love doesn't torment people forever.

Perfect love doesn't guilt you into obedience.

Perfect love doesn't demand a credit card and a confession.

Perfect love says:
> *"You're already enough.*
>
> *You're already wanted.*
>
> *You don't have to be afraid anymore."*

And that's the gospel worth saving.

Reclaiming It - Chapter 1:
If Jesus Walked Into Your Church Today

If Jesus walked into your church today, would anyone even recognize him?

Not the image — not stained glass Jesus with the blow-dried hair and glowing robe.

The real one.

Brown-skinned.

Dust on his feet.

Wearing no title.

Asking hard questions.

Would the greeters welcome him?

Would the pastor hand him the mic?

Would the church leadership sit him down — or ask him to leave?

Because here's what he probably wouldn't do:
- He wouldn't head straight for the stage.
- He wouldn't ask about the building fund.
- He wouldn't be impressed by the sound system or the crowd size.
- He wouldn't compliment the branding.

He'd be looking for the ones no one's paying attention to.

He Wouldn't Fit the Brand

He wouldn't speak in polished sermon quotes.

He wouldn't tell you you're "blessed and highly favored."

He wouldn't push books or post reels.

He'd ask why the homeless are kept out of the sanctuary.

He'd ask why women still can't lead.

He'd ask why the poor are blamed for their poverty.

He'd ask why the sermon sounds more like a TED Talk than a gospel.

And if you tried to explain that "we do things a little differently here,"

he'd probably flip a few things over — again.

And What Would We Do?

Would we listen to him?

Or would we accuse him of being divisive?

Would we call him a prophet?

Or call him "too political"?

Would we tweet his quotes?

Or walk out when he preached forgiveness for your enemies?

If he called out your church's obsession with money — would you say amen… or unfollow?

If he called out your pastor's celebrity status — would you nod… or get defensive?

Because here's the truth:

If Jesus walked into most churches today, he wouldn't be preaching.

He'd be interrupting.

But Here's the Real Question:

Would You Follow Him?

The real him.

Not the one your church approves of.

Not the one your favorite author quotes.

Not the brand ambassador version.

Would you follow the Jesus who says:
- Sell your stuff.
- Forgive people who don't deserve it.
- Love your enemies.
- Sit with the broken.
- Call out religious hypocrisy.
- Give up your seat.
- Let the last go first.

Because that's the one who flipped history.

And he didn't do it from a pulpit.

Reclaiming It - Chapter 2:
The Message Is Still Good

I'm not a "Christian."

Not anymore.

I grew up in it.

I played the songs.

I sat through the sermons.

I memorized the verses.

I even went to a Lutheran college where they made us study theology — and that's when the cracks started to show.

Not because I became angry or bitter or lost.

But because I started to pay attention.

Because once you really look at what Jesus actually said…

and compare it to what's being done in his name…

you can't unsee it.

And once you've seen it, you've got a choice:

Walk away from all of it…

or dig deeper to see if there's anything worth saving.

I Think There Is

There's something underneath all the noise.

All the performance.

All the empire.

All the shame.

All the fear.

There's something still beating down there — quiet, but alive.

It's not the church.

It's not the institution.

It's not the brand.

It's the message.

And the message is still good.

It Was Always Meant to Be Simple

Love people.

Feed the hungry.

Sit with the broken.

Tell the truth.

Call out injustice.

Forgive what you thought was unforgivable.

And never believe you're better than anyone else.

That's it.

That's what the man in sandals was trying to show us.

Before emperors twisted it.

Before churches sold it.

Before politicians hijacked it.

Before shame covered it up.

Strip it down — and the message still stands.

You Don't Have to Be Religious to See the Value

You don't have to believe in heaven to want justice now.

You don't have to believe in hell to be kind.

You don't have to subscribe to doctrine to know that love changes things.

You don't need to be "saved" to see what's sacred.

You just need a heart that's open.

And a mind that's not afraid to ask, "What if this isn't about religion at all?"

What If God Is Bigger Than the System Built to Contain Him?

What if the church missed the point?

What if the gatekeepers don't have the keys?

What if Jesus can still be found — just not where they told you to look?

Not in buildings that sell salvation.

Not in sermons that demand perfection.

Not in fear. Not in shame. Not in pride.

But in small things.

In quiet honesty.

In justice.

In love that costs something.

In a rebel from Nazareth who was killed for saying:

"The last will be first."

"You are forgiven."

"You are already enough."

You're Allowed to Believe in That

Even if you don't go to church.

Even if you don't have all the answers.

Even if you're angry.

Even if you've walked away.

Even if you never go back.

You can still believe in something true, something good, and something worth following — even if it doesn't have a label.

Because Jesus wasn't offering religion.

He was offering a way to live.

And that way still works.

Even if you have to dig through centuries of noise to find it.

Faith isn't the problem. Religion isn't the enemy.

Christianity — at its core — is not what's broken.

What's broken is the version that got hijacked. The one that traded grace for guilt, love for leverage, and truth for tribalism.

There are good churches. There are good pastors. There are communities doing it right — feeding people, healing wounds, holding space for those in need.

They're out there. They're just harder to hear over the noise.

The New Testament never says, "Go to church."

It says, "Don't give up on meeting together."

It says, "Love one another."

It says, "Where two or three gather, I'm there."

The problem isn't gathering.

The problem is when the gathering becomes a performance.

When faith becomes a brand.

When "church" becomes more about seating charts, stage lighting, and revenue than about humility and healing.

This book isn't anti-Christian.

It's anti-fake Christianity.

Anti-Corruption.

And if you've ever felt like you didn't belong in the version you were handed… maybe it's because that version didn't belong to Jesus in the first place.

I'm not a "Christian."

Not anymore.

And honestly?

I don't think Jesus would be either.

Reclaiming It – Chapter Three:
Heaven on Earth

Jesus didn't come to start a religion.

He came to free people from it.

He didn't say build temples or join a denomination.

He said, "The Kingdom of God is within you."

But we couldn't hear it — we were too human.

Too busy. Too proud. Too afraid.

We turned his voice into doctrine.

His love into law.

His presence into performance.

He never asked for a building.

He never demanded rituals.

He didn't want our guilt — he wanted our awareness.

> "Let those with ears, hear."

He was speaking to the soul, not the system.

But we kept showing up with checklists waiting for permission to be worthy.

And all the while, he was whispering:

You already are.

This isn't something you can be taught.
It's something that breaks through.
It's not handed to you — it's something you remember.
It's not carved in stone or printed in a book.
It's written in silence.
And when it rises, you don't need anyone to explain it.
You just know.

Jesus spoke in riddles because truth can't be spoon-fed.
It has to awaken.
And when it does, it changes everything.

"You will know the truth, and the truth will set you free."

Not save you.
Free you.

But religion doesn't want you free.
It wants you obedient.
Tithing. Performing. Apologizing for being human.

Because the moment you realize heaven was never "out there,"
the whole system collapses.

Heaven isn't a reward.

It's a realization.

It's not streets of gold.

It's this moment — the one between the silence of birth and the silence of death —

when you become conscious enough to feel it.

To know it.

To live like nothing can be taken from you,

because nothing ever truly belonged to you anyway.

Jesus didn't say, "Be Christian."

He said, "Follow me."

And when people asked where the kingdom was, he said:

"It doesn't come by observation.

You won't say, 'Here it is,' or 'There it is.'

The Kingdom of God is within you."

— Luke 17:20–21

He wasn't painting a picture of the afterlife.

He was describing a state of being. A way of seeing. A shift in awareness.

We missed it because we were too focused on getting into heaven

to realize it was already trying to get into us.

So maybe this was never about religion.
Maybe it's about spiritual clarity.

It's what happens when ego dissolves and love takes over.
When we stop judging, stop clinging, stop hoarding power and pain.

Heaven is a condition of the soul — not a prize for following rules.

It's about stepping outside the noise long enough to hear the truth underneath all of it:

You are not broken.
You are not separate.
You are not owned.
You are already standing on holy ground.

And when you know that — truly know it —
no one can sell you your freedom ever again.

That's heaven on earth.
And it's been here the whole time.

And Jesus wasn't the only one who saw it.

People like the Buddha, Lao Tzu, Rumi, Meister Eckhart, and Teresa of Ávila all reached for the same light — outside religion, beyond systems, deeper than doctrine.

They didn't want to be worshiped.
They wanted to wake people up.

And once you wake up,
you stop trying to get to heaven
and start living like it's already here.

Epilogue:
The God of Death

There was a time when people believed the sun was a god, because they didn't understand it.

The moon. The stars. The water. The wind. Earthquakes. Thunder.

Anything mysterious was sacred. Divine.

And as science peeled back those mysteries — explained the solar system, the weather, the biology of life — one by one, the "gods" vanished.

But one still remains.

Death.

We don't know what happens after. No microscope can show us.
No telescope can zoom in.
And so, for many people, that last mystery still belongs to God.

Not because it's proven. But because it's the only explanation that makes them feel okay.

God of the gaps, yes. But more than that — God of the ending. God of the exit.

And for a lot of people, that's enough reason to believe. Just in case.

But what if faith was more than a safety net? What if hope wasn't a backup plan? What if the way we live — right now — mattered more than what happens when we die?

Final Thoughts

The idea of the God of Death started as a final paper I wrote in my last theology class in college. I didn't know how it would land.

I got an A.

And one note from the professor:

"Keep exploring."

And I have been — ever since.

Because the questions never stopped.

Not about God. Not about faith.

Not about what we've built in his name — or what we've broken.

The New Testament talks about the end.

Wars. Deception. Love growing cold.

But Jesus didn't tell us to panic.

He told us to love.

To forgive. To feed.

To show up for people — even the ones who didn't deserve it.

Especially them.

Because faith isn't the problem.

Religion isn't the enemy.

Christianity — at its core — isn't what's broken.

What's broken is the version that used fear to control,

shame to silence,

and power to protect itself.

There are still good people.

Still real faith.

Still sacred spaces where love leads.

Jesus didn't build walls.

He built a table.

He welcomed the ones religion left behind.

He broke the rules that kept people out.

He didn't require perfection — just presence.

And maybe he wasn't perfect the way religion sells it.

Maybe he was better.

Real. Human. Honest. Brave enough to weep, bold enough to challenge power, and still loving enough to forgive the people who killed him.

And if that's who God is —

if there is one —

maybe there's still hope for all of us.

www.ingramcontent.com/pod-product-compliance
Lightning Source LLC
Chambersburg PA
CBHW030448100526
44580CB00002B/38